The River Within

poems

Ann Taylor

The River Within is the winner of the inaugural
Cathlamet Prize for Poetry offered by Ravenna Press.

cover image courtesy of Kathleen Krueger

ISBN: 978-0-9835982-8-2
LCCN: 2011933802

Published by Ravenna Press
Spokane, Washington
USA
www.ravennapress.com

FIRST EDITION

"Mountain mastiffs and hungry shepherds;"
An Introduction

For its inaugural Cathlamet Prize for Poetry in 2011 (the winner of which you now hold in your hand), Ravenna Press picked American poet Lynn Strongin as sole judge to select from the fine array of manuscripts submitted to the contest inaugurated to note publication of our 55th title and our dozen years of publishing. To a press with a reputation not just for promoting fine and serious work anchored in strong literary foundations, but also for its experimental bent and innovative inclinations, Strongin brought a confident hand to sort through an amazing variety of styles and material and ultimately select a solid, appealing work that bore some relations to the Press' own roots. A long-time resident of British Columbia, Strongin was "discovered" in the 1960s by Denise Levertov when a section of a long poem electrified her and led to Levertov's nominating Strongin for inclusion in her first anthology *31 New American Poets* (Ed. Ron Schreiber, Hill & Wang, NY, 1969). Strongin has since gone on to produce many books in her own strong, imagistic and highly personal style, including a Ravenna title in 2010: *Twin Tan Dogs, Obedience & Discipline.* "Basically," she has said, speaking out of her own experience with childhood polio, "the body is a house with a lot of windows, but no door you can go out." Perhaps it was the willingness of another poet to look out and consider a very far-ranging field indeed that most drew her to Ann Taylor's poetry, a line of which is quoted for the title of this Introduction.

Taylor is another poet who has paid her dues, in her case in the halls of education, putting degrees from Northeastern and Boston Universities to work at Salem State University for many years, teaching a variety of courses in literature and writing, a broad sweep that includes surveys of Arthurian Literature. Alternating between an elegiacal and a light hand in *The River Within*, Dr. Taylor considers an internalized, time-deep, history-rich outside: from Darwin and Walpole to family (she and her husband have a son and daughter), cats & dogs; from Annie Oakley and Cleopatra to Sam Spade to Methuselah; from Paris to Masai Mara, Oxford to the Moon; and from the Library of Assurbanipal to her own contemporary students. This range of reference—enhanced by her family's own international travels and supported by a reasonable life which includes bird watching and features the inspirations of Cape Cod in the starkest days of winter—forms and informs the many threads of her work and life. She shares them in this book, all movements of the river within.

Those threads must have influenced selection of this surprisingly appropriate book. The Cathlamet Prize was named for a small town on the Columbia River, on the Washington State side, a confluence during the 1800s for indigenous tribes, explorers, traders, trappers and merchants and, steadily over time, early white settlers, so many from Scandinavia and Europe with all those histories in tow.

> they trace their paths,
> backbone thin,
> aligned like *cordilleras*.
>
> (from "Hypotenuses")

Ravenna Editor Rantala's family of Finnish immigrants in the early 1900's traveled from Varkus and Pyhajoki to Toronto, to San Francisco, to Astoria, Oregon, to Puget Island in the Columbia River (a few miles up from its mouth, able to reach Cathlamet only by boat until dedication of the new bridge in 1939) then into Cathlamet. See Taylor's title poem:

Wind draws ocean to desert,
          shapes clouds that flood islands out.

In my once-a-field, now-sinkhole pond, snappers
          claw mud, moist with the Queen's Nile,

hooded by ice that sank the Titanic –
          spring risings, crystal descents.

The Prize honors all those (and everything they bring with them) who reach out to encounter a world.

"This was an exciting contest to judge," said judge Strongin. "There was consistent high quality in the offerings. Each collection of poems had a voice of its own. The dominant music was, for me, somewhat elegiac. The images weave their own backdrop as we hold our breaths, spiritually, at the start of the second decade of this millennium. All song traces its way back and arises from the river that runs within us. Call it our hunger, our yearning, it occurs within the voiced love and lament accompanying all ceremonies of letting go."

We hope you enjoy the book.

The Editors,
Ravenna Press

Table of Contents

Part I

Part II

Part III

for my mother again

The River Within

The river is within us, the sea is all about us;
The sea is the land's edges also, the granite
Into which it reaches, the beaches where it tosses
Its hints of earlier and other creation . . .

T.S. Eliot, "The Dry Salvages"

Part I

The River Within

Triceratops washes down volcano dust
        with what I'm sipping now

or with today's Ganges, floating
        a shrouded body to a new birth.

Wind draws ocean to desert,
        shapes clouds that flood islands out.

In my once-a-field, now-sinkhole pond, snappers
        claw mud, moist with the Queen's Nile,

hooded by ice that sank the Titanic –
        spring risings, crystal descents.

Let There Be Moose

On the first day, in the slant light of sunset,
one startles, lifts a heavy head,
eyes the idling car from the forest edge.

Crossing the road just after,
another cuts a quick silhouette
through pink dusk,
skids down the embankment,
drinks the gutter's rich runoff.

Deep in green, a tall one
gnaws long reeds dripping,
as darkness transforms
sky to seascape, clouds to rocky islands –
until they all dissolve to black.

On what could be the fourth,
a young one wanders obscured
by the clearing's new growth –
antlers velvety, short of autumn's
tines and palmates. Evening sparks
summer stars, and throned Cassiopeia
anticipates the moon.

Off a noon trail, rustling in dry grass,
hint of bear, a bog duck-busy, blackbird trills,

fish surfacing and splashing, a shriek,
enough to spook this wary one into the firs,
leaving loons riding the ripples.

Near the paved lot,
in evening shadow
of the public-works sign
forbidding moose-watching,
the last lingers,

this day done.

Annie Oakley: Peerless Lady Wing-Shot

I can shoot the head off
a running quail,
pop an apple
from between my
dog's ears, fire ashes
from cigarettes held
between a daredevil's lips,
split playing cards edgewise,
backward through a mirror.

I make targets
while hurdling
a tabletop
or galloping bareback.

I also fancy my chestnut mane,
dainty slipper shoes,
embroidered skirts, necklaces
strung with prize medals.

Frank Butler was a fair shot,
but I beat him by one hit,
made him my attendant
in Buffalo Bill's show,
married him fifty years.

He's the one who tosses
just right those glass balls,
clay pigeons for me to blast.

He doesn't think much
of my housekeeping,
but still loves
my smoky, quick-lever
repeating action.

Cleopatra's Conquest

"Where's the bronze donkey bearing
baskets of fresh olives, and the sturgeon
delivered by slaves fingering flutes?

Where are the flamingo tongues,
ostrich heads, milk-fattened snails,
hares winged like Pegasus?"

Mark Antony mocked, nibbling
the plain pancake, chicken leg,
dessert fig placed before him.

"And where the other twenty-one courses,
the jesters, jugglers, revolving ceiling,
the sprinkler's subtle perfume?"

"Call me the Queen of Plenty," she replied,
announcing her aim to devour
the most lavish meal ever all by herself.

She removed her huge pearl earring,
the largest in history, a king's treasure,
richer than all Roman banquets combined,

dropped it into her cup of wine vinegar,
and as it sizzled
drank it.

Only Annual

The spring's big night has come and gone. I'm late
for salamanders, vernal pools again,
the muck and mud, just right on that one date.

Occupied, I chose my usual fate,
missing this one-time vital digging in.
The spring's big night has come and gone. I'm late,

unlike Housman, knowing cherries abate,
who wouldn't let his blooms become has-beens,
so hiked through muck and mud's ideal dates.

I missed the yellow-spotteds' single night
just as before, my inattentive sin,
while spring's big night arrived, departed. Late,

I didn't catch their marching, congregate,
their frolic, matching, digging to begin
in muck and mud, set for this single date.

Next year, I'm sure, I'll note their plans to mate,
delay my work, determined to take in
the spring's big night for which I won't be late,
alert to muck and mud on that one date.

Jenny and Charles

How she ended up in a child's flannel nightie
on the wrong side of the bars, ogled daily
by Londoners in frills, top hats, and tails,

and why this balding cagemate with bushy sideburns
watched her every move, scratched notebooks,
she couldn't figure out.

Darwin was entranced with Jenny,
housed himself with her, smiled, and wrote
when she threw a tantrum for an apple,

placed his gift of a mouth organ straight
to her lips, astonished herself
with her own image in a mirror.

At home, he was happier still to record
whatever she and his children had in common –
their monkeyshines, her humanness.

Collectors

Whatever cup, coin, ivory comb,
rhino-hide shield, Turkish dagger,
Cardinal's hat moved him, Walpole
housed at Strawberry Hill.

Crazed photo of a stranger, a cockatoo,
blue sand, broken compass, dice,
Cornell framed in small 3-D boxes
on Utopia.

Both captured the sphere's movement –
one in a Renaissance gilt clock,
the other in a rusty watch
without hands.

A hurt, a joy, a notion, a newsclip,
snippet of talk, iambic echo,
sound attuned, digitized moments falling,
set in stanzas here on Pistol Hill.

Still Life with Empty Bowl

The birds, cows, fish, galloping horses especially
        will be way past their frames,
                if, late again, you don't get here soon.

        Don't you know that Mycerinus and his queen
                will have taken their step?
        That red lanterns will likely be extinguished,
                robed guests standing, stretching,
                        strolling downriver beneath China trees,

and John will no doubt be fetching his gift-fruit,
        tossed by the Christ-child across the room?
St. Francis' prayer will be done,
        he off to breakfast . . . or heaven.

Degas' ballerina will already be twirling on stage,
        and Georgia O'Keeffe's lily begun its wilt.

Oh sure, the guards will remain stationed,
fingers clasped behind their backs,

        but you'd better hope that Paul Revere
        is still pondering his silver pot,
        that the picnickers haven't packed it up,
        that hourglasses, sundials, grandfather clocks
        got stalled in their moment,
        and that the melting watch
        hasn't splattered
        to the floor.

Hypotenuses

Ruling their diagonals across
the village square, Pujayo's night cats
might please Pythagoras.

From my balcony, I watch one draw
straight into red bracts of bougainvillea,
another through the slapping cat door

into the stable, then one direct
to the shade behind the crumbling fountain.
Mountain mastiffs and hungry shepherds

snore and growl, guard cottage doors,
wait for just one cat to swerve. But no,
old slaughters have taught them to resist

all itches, urges, deviations.
Legs blurred into skirts, angles elegant,
lines crossed in central bursts of motion,

they trace their paths,
backbone thin,
aligned like *cordilleras*.

Parade-bone

With her retriever's soft bite,
she nightly hoists her rawhide bone
like a barbell, snuffles a route
along the couch, around the hassock,
past the bookcase, pausing only
to dance out the fire
of the living room rug.

When she noses my fingers,
I give her a required pat,
pitch a convincing thank-you,
receive her gift slowly,
her jaws relaxed,
my hands easy on the knobs.

Did her forebears patrol
the carnivore's cave-blaze,
stamp out vagrant flames,
share the spoils?
Did some gentle Tristan, mail reflecting
firelight, practice this knightly courtesy?
Did Labrador angler hand back her fish,
Victorian gunman her partridge?

She stares, expects
my overwrought gratitude,

accepts my obedient return
of her loan, proceeds
until, a nest spun into her bed,
she sleeps, bone under the piano,
at paw's reach.

Red Cat, Clyde

He's all Outback – no seal-point
Himalayan, but red,
even to the insides of his ears,
sore paws padding crimson dust
down hospital halls.

At Cloncurry, his nurse-rescuer knew
nothing of his cruise from Tasmania curled
in a spiral of deck ropes, nothing of his
three-year, two-thousand-mile odyssey.

He couldn't describe highway wheels
swerving at him, nor could she
hear dingoes' howling.
She couldn't see him napping
with koalas in eucalyptus, stalking
birds, frogs, rabbits, rats,
gasping through smothering dust,
outsmarting that sneaky Inland Taipan.

She wouldn't understand that even
after her vet found the ID chip,
after they flew him free back to Tas –
to love, two squares, a bed,
worldwide fame –
he's nosing into the reporter's
stuffed duffel, escaping.
But he is.

Finding the Hidden Meaning

"This is impossible," she complains,
angry at words that don't add up.

Another guesses, fears he's wrong,
"Why can't they *say*
what they're thinking?"

"The poet's not the Easter Bunny,"
I answer. Poets don't write
straight then stash meanings
under thorny shrubs
just to make things harder.
Reading takes practice, an open mind,
faith in the poem . . . and yourself.

They don't see it,
even when I help them
stock their baskets.

Spectral

They put down their books, end the course, at last,
my students done, they think, and on their way –
but I go beside them, their reading ghost.

They think they're surely free of Pope and Frost.
But they're wrong. I haunt, interrupt their play.
So what if books are shut, course done, at last?

I fan pages to ones I cherish most,
chant passages, possessing them to stay.
I charm them, their persistent reading ghost.

I highlight perfect lines, otherwise lost,
stir memories that might've got away,
though books seem shut, and they released at last.

I summon texts that they unwisely tossed,
push their continued reading, night and day,
assigning still, their bossy reading ghost.

Perhaps our paths are done with being crossed,
but I trip them up, never far astray.
As they shut their books, end the course at last,
I am, I hope, their lifelong reading ghost.

Annie Taylor Takes the Falls

Harnessed into a four-and-a-half-foot
Kentucky oak hooped barrel, she rocked
through Niagara's upper rapids,
hurtled herself
over the Horseshoe Falls –
one hundred seventy feet
straight
down.

Over sixty,
a teacher of math,
tired of ciphering
and hell bent on fame,
she took seventeen minutes –
forever the first
to dare the dive,
the dash to death
on rocks.

"No one ought ever do *that* again!"
she warned, quaking,
propped from rapids across a shaky ramp –

a "Queen of the Mist,"
numbered forever in the company
of daredevils.

Part II

Methuselah

roots in a blasted dolomite plot
at eleven thousand feet.

Diminutive, gnarly,
this bristlecone looks down
on clockless Las Vegas,
drinks rare snow-water,
heats in desiccating sun,
a thin strip of bark standing
between life and firewood.

Each year, slim needs trim
still further
while the
youngest growth
draws all energy,
staking real estate
with a five-thousand-year lease – renewable.

Water, sun, provident bark,
and a sprig of green to tend to.

Friday Night for Sale

We spun wobbly piano stools,
scrambled over Flexible Flyers,
squeezed behind peacock-feathered
room dividers, pawed warped Perry Como's,
rusty forks, monogrammed towels,
and, yellowed flounces flattened,
the wedding gown itself.

Fidgety between my parents,
toes fanning sawdust,
I looked up to old hay stringing
barn lofts like uncombed hair,
and acrobatic light bulbs on long wires,
waited for Joe to auction
something I could want.

Holding up the splotched mirror
framed with cracked pink seashells,
he inquired, "Now what'm I gonna get
for *this* little beauty?"

He placed the past in the future –
the tarnished gold stallion/clock combo,
"t' get y'all here on time,"
the "tuneful" plunk
of the violin's one string,

that gown for the lucky gal
who'd be "pretty as a picture
on her special day."

In the car going home,
I tried and tried
to rub a promised luster
into my very own, one-dollar,
"sure-to-impress-all-comers,"
solid brass doorknob.

Pencil

"Say five Hail Marys" –
my first-confession penance
for my "I-stole-ten-pencils" sin.

My next pencil may be a catalog's
quality graphite, woodsy green,
encased, it says, in incense-cedar,
sure to emit with every message
a subtle fragrance.

I read that a pencil can write 45,000 words,
draw a line thirty-five miles long –
consume itself
with its own verbosity.

Mine never neared these distances.
I chewed them,
piercing smooth bark,
grinding deep to splinter,
then to softened pulp
at the dark core.

Less hungry, I love them still –
my glittery red stocking-stuffer
rolling to me across the desk,
my husband's just-sharpened

hexagonal yellow at the phone,
the one touting in green script
down its side a challenging
Dixon Ticonderoga 1388-3H, HARD

Custom-Made

My aunt's fingers nudged too close
to the wild thug and tug
of the industrial needle,
as she zip-stitched seams
for wingbacks, curvaceous ottomans,
shaped any couch in an hour.

In our house's downstairs workroom,
she apprenticed me.
I was a fair cutter, a trimmer,
but beyond the predictability of cording,
a stitcher far too wary
of the machine's bucking will.

At my college tuition time,
its midnight roar too often
awakened me, the extra
that allowed me to flee that sound,
the needle's prick, the late-night's
labor, and try my hand at this stitchery.

Julia's Leonids

I kept her awake
to hear wolves howl
in the Canada night,

or I helped her trace
an eclipse's crescent
moonshapes on hardtop.

Tonight, I ruffle
an empty comforter.
She's already at her window.
"Look!" she whispers,
"Let's go out."

I stumble down the stairs
to the lawn. Dew seeps
between the toes
of my slipper socks.

As a falling star burns out,
I remember lifting her
to follow the comet's tail
in the tottering scope.

"If you want, you can go in now,"
she announces.
I shiver in the dampness, stay.

Coins of the Realm

My father loved money, not Everyman's
never-shared *Goods* hoarded sinfully in corners,
but the clink and the heft of it,

the clatter and schush of the Sunday collection
basket he served down the aisle, the sleight
of numismatic shows' bargainers and crooks,

the mail coin auctions, where he let me sort
the "Very Fines," from the worn-down "Fairs,"
and keep his weighty loose-leaf records of bids.

He was a banker, "Sam Spade" to the tellers
he trained to spy the false names, the lying
picture ID's with add-on glasses and wigs.

His vacations were slot-poker-blackjack Vegas,
a win an extra Elvis movie for my sister and me,
an ice cream smoothie on the Strip.

His weekends were beaches, his metal detector
tattling on coins burrowed beneath the hardpan
or retrieving rings for careless sunbathers.

In his study, after his last heart attack, I hugged
the brand new detector, the one he had assembled
that day and had tested for me hours before,

coming up with nothing beneath the driveway
pavement. The instructions open on his desk
promised a deeper reach, a long-lived battery.

At the Divide

I expected something grander, more Red Sea,
    but Isa Lake, stalled green with lily pads,
seems more inclined to merge, to blossom huge
    and yellow, than to proceed, though at eight
thousand feet, the Continental Divide's imaginary line
    nearly palpable, in capitals, droplets must head

either west, down a rocky cliff to the Snake,
    then maybe to a quick ride on a cyclist's helmet,
a skateboard to Malibu and the warm Pacific,
    or east, for a longer haul to the Yellowstone
then by freight or river barge, for a rough ride
    to the stormy Atlantic gulf.

In heavy rain, the only apparent action, I follow
    a streamlet down the windshield
and finally to the pavement where it pools, meanders,
    slips into Isa, rebel Isa, technically compliant
like a teen's apology, but delivering waters contrary,
    the west side east, the east west.

Je ne sais quoi

"You have a Parisian instep,"
said the old war vet
professor in my new department,
admiring the style
of my stride,
high on spike heels.

Preferring my time seamless,
I don't ache with nostalgia.
I'm more irked than festive
on New Year's Eve.
My hours are not punctuated
by my clock's cuckoo,
strangled years ago.

Today, safe in sensible flats
with corrugated soles,
I watch my daughter set off
for her new job, stylish
across ice, on shiny black spikes,
and I'm surprised by my longing
for another chance to be taken
for some walker on a Paris street.

Campsite at Masai Mara

A fanged snarl. A streak
of scarred beige quivers
away flies, a tail twitches
electric to its tip. A wrinkly
yawn, a breathy
pause out of view.
Clawed paws pad,
stir dust –
never all whole,
but small frames
through the twelve-inch mesh
tent window where I keep watch.

Heat ripples pink
across the long horizon,
thorn-trees deepen in silhouette,
hundreds of wildebeest grunt,
almost consoling,
until a death-shriek,
and another, opens
my night of no words,
no motion, no sleep.

Vaulted roars, rhythmic pants –
lionesses, maybe three, maybe more,
circle the campsite in the dusk.

In blackness, a slice of starscape
becomes visible through the mesh,
Jimi Hendrix riffs float
from the stone guardhouse.
A lioness growls discontent,
paws our dowsed fire.

In gray dawn's silence,
a nearby thorn bows
under Lappet-faced vultures,
breast feathers matted.

So much of my journeying has been with you,

it's hard to recall a place without you
placed within it – you a shadow ahead
on the Oxford towpath's night trail,
sure-footed, no flashlight,

you far across the Alpine saddleback
balancing wine and cheese
on the melting glacier.

You with your worn *Blue Guide*,
pacing the hot Parthenon to locate
Athena's sacred olive.

My memories of Kenya bring you
tugging my camera from the robber monkey,
your breadknife protecting our tent
from the lion roaring just feet away.

My Taj shadows you in and out
through soft moonlight,
my Great Wall, you running the steps –

all more regarded than my own being there,
than the place itself.

The Lagoon

A palette of rust – giltless goldenrod,
sticky burrs, fallen acorns broken,
cat-o'-nine-tails, ragged like bucks' antlers
shedding velvet.
                    Cracked milkweed pods
clinging like wounded birds, a few feathery filaments
waiting to break loose.
                    Abandoned nests exposed on bare limbs,
remaining leaves countable,
the rest hustling down cracked pavement,
or waved to water's edge, soon to be frozen under.

But still, tight white birch catkins, like raindrops
suspended, seeded.
Wispy young pines rooted in the esker.
Chickadees' persistent comment in the cold air,
coots bobbing, mallards still paired,
swan parents circling with offspring ready for flight,
a noisy flurry of Canada Geese, chaotic, agreeing
only on south.
The warm sun's slight heat.

Today's harvesting chipmunk, like me,
anticipating, faithful to the mostly unseen.

Tracings

of snowbird, mallard, squirrel,
pockmarks of melting drops,

my own big boots, but not yet
the trill of redwings,

their swaying on cattails now
only a long memory, or foreseen.

An hourglass of open water crowded
with gulls away from the sea,

a storm coming. Near-weightless coots
tempting ice vanishing thin at the edges.

Rabbit tracks stopped where yesterday
the hawk watched, and reflected maple

limbs reaching, airbrushed, across the snow.
Then someone's memorial wreath,

and a small square of turf chained off,
embracing a stone for another. My tracks

behind me, and in late sun, my shadow
stretching down the evergreen trail.

Near Athens

A coffee-cup Greek temple with a single stone
centered upright on a driftwood plinth,
a stick of seaweed thumbed into the damp,
Athena's olive. This he raised on a sand acropolis.

When he joined a kids' tumbling
paddleball game, I wanted to protect
his sacred precinct, until a spinning missile
scudded low, toppled a leaning column,
brought down the heights.

Returning to the windy café where I waited,
he stumbled across the ruins.
I put down my guidebook,
promised less time with the ancients,
more beach for the next day,
as I watched him nudge black olives
around a plate's circumference,
prop up at the center a white chunk
of feta cheese.

When You Have Forgotten Oxford

(after Gwendolyn Brooks)

And when you have forgotten the year of days at the library,
and most especially
when you have forgotten the late afternoons –
when you have forgotten the fading light
when we crossed to the *Eagle and Child,* or
me with a pint, sitting in C. S. Lewis's chair, you in Tolkien's.

When you have forgotten hoping for inspiration,
me worrying why I set my dissertation in the Middle Ages,
wondering who in this world might care about Gualterus.

And how you listened closely when the pub got noisy.
And how happy I was when you got it, approved.

And how we then set out for the cottage,
down the two-mile canal towpath in the dark,
voles splashing, making way for us, unexpected,
quiet cows encroaching across the fields,
the aroma of coal hearths as we neared the village
eager to fire up our own.

I say, when you have forgotten that,
when you have forgotten how much you remember,
how much the year became our lives,
and how before the flame, we finally put down our Dickens
like some dozy Victorians,
lay on the braided rug warm till the coals burned out.

When you have, I say, forgotten all that,
I'll know we're no longer here –
no heavenly fire so heated,
no celestial rug such a comfort.

Take the Hills

My mother grew up among them –
Misery, Rag, Shag, her own Pistol –
despite the names, mostly neighborly.

She hiked them to town, skied another,
climbed one for Boston fireworks,
drove unaware over others.

But Sunday, from an icy incline
near church, she was guided
by her own First Communicants.

"Too busy for a broken hip,"
she announced, continuing her climb
every day before I'm awake.

Part III

Almost

It's a little off tonight,
 not like the full moon of June's spoon
 or the one the cow jumped over.
  Not like the scimitar crescent slicing
   its portion of the night sky, nor the harvest moon
   presiding over the final corn crop,
    pumpkins' rotundity. Nor the once-in-a-blue moon.
   Not the scientists' retreating moon in orbit,
    leaving us by an inch and a half a year,
     but still tugging reliably at the tides.
    Nor the poets' moon signifying everything
     from love's swooning, to youth's loss,
      to God's grace, to life's inconstancy,
      to silver for the most common landscape.
     No, this moon inclines to roundness,
      but asymmetric at the rim, neither
      a sharp cut at the half nor a picturesque
     arc. It's "gibbous," or "humped," "swollen,"
     imperfect, a little off,
     most of the time.

Children's Garden

Snowdrop, Blackthorn, Halcyon –
paths where gusts eddy
reds and golds
around mossy stones –

dearest child,
most beloved,
sweetest one –

Party-dressed,
attended by an angel,
a small girl
precious gift
clenches her long fingers
made for prayer,
bows her head.

A plump infant,
arms outstretched,
lifts straight
on a pillow cloud
to heaven's cumulus –

our miracle,
parents' hope,
lent, not given –

Rain now weighs
leaves down,
and from the tip
of a kneeling boy's
finely-sculpted nose,
huge droplets swell,
grow heavy,
fall to the book
he's hugged
a century long.

Staffordshire Burial

The gold snout tapers trimly,
neck stretched, as if reaching across
thirteen hundred years for a caress.

A horse's head with incised harness,
hand-sized, polished smooth,
it speaks of goldsmith's craft,
of beauty beyond any warrior need,
of peace's grace.

In antlered hall in glittering candlelight,
Wealtheow pours mead, the *comitatus* convenes,
the *geldwine* offers gifts as thanks,
the *scop* strokes the lyre, sings just-done deeds

just before the jumble of a quick stashing
underground among decorated crosses,
gemmed rings, carved cheekpieces,

just before raiders rip doors off frames,
tip the tables, take the women,
feed again the great hall to flames.

"The fear of death is upon the child"
(after Andrea Rico di Candia's "Virgin of the Passion")

Robed rich in red, gilt-framed, haloed,
you receive no hug,
no playful pull at your veil. You hold
no little king upright on your lap,
nor do you nurse him, rosy-cheeked,
balance him on your *contrapposto* hip,
or caress his curly hair.

Yes, you prop him up, incline your head,
but he looks away this time,
turns back awkward to archangels hovering,
Gabriel bearing four nails, the cross,
Michael a jug of vinegar, a sponge.

One fine sandal dangles loose,
as he clings with both hands
to your upraised thumb.

The inscription speaks not for him alone.
In your large eyes, familiar dread –
the siren slicing the night,
the shatter of shells, the police officer,
two formal soldiers, a reluctant knock
at the door.

En Paz Descanse

Deiá, Majorca

"Robert's grave," laughed the tourguides,
once amusing the poet himself.

Now the grave is a sunbaked slab,
uneven on weedy, disruptive soil.
Scraggy succulents gnaw the edges,
a white jar of worn flowers at the head,
with a dead red candle in a pot.

At the foot, a line of small wooden crosses,
pinned with aging poppies from his
Welsh Fusiliers to Captain Graves.

The grave's like him, unsettled:
 translator, historian, biographer, critic,
 novelist, lecturer, essayist, poet – restless.

Reviser, romantic realist, whimsical cynic,
aesthete of contradictions, this Majorcan Englishman,
worldly villager, wanted no bronze
"to dribble green in times of rain,"
no marble.

Just jagged cursive – the name, the dates,
the *EPD*, and centered,
the singular task that mattered,
set firmly in the sun –

POETA

The Prince Frog

When the spiteful fairy cursed me,
the last thing I foresaw was bliss.
But I've come to love the oozy slime
between my toes, the slip and slop
of heaving myself to the next pad.
It's all luscious, a green easy
to get into, not those gleaming greaves,
breastplates clanking, always-rusting
princely stuff. Here I breathe
deep, suck in rich muck scent
of swamp rot, and gurgle with my mates
among white lilies. From underneath,
I spy with telescope eyes.
                                        Oh, no!

Here comes the fumblethumb princess,
always losing her golden ball.
A faint whisper tells me to beg
a kiss – just one, it always says.
Why would I do that? My perfect
match is here, plump, lubricious,
responsive to my croaks,
herself full-lipped,
and well along in spawning.

She can fetch herself
another retriever, a willing kisser,
leave me with my ever after.

Cloaks, Italia

"Misericordia,"
the merciful virgin is called.

In the gallery, supplicants, hands pressed
in prayer, huddle within her mantle.
Glowing in heaven's gold, she grows
monumental, embraces saint and sinner alike.

A hawk mantling prey, he swoops
down the dark sidewalk,
flashes open his overcoat lined
with priced photos of come-hither nudes.

Spotting police, he closes down, snarls,
"Maledizione!"

The Library of Assurbanipal

Seeking fame for learning, the king assembled
his collection from across the ancient world,

ordered scribes to carve texts in cuneiform tablets,
set up colossal stone human-headed lions,

eagle-headed humans, eagle-winged bulls,
and stationed self-sacrificing eunuchs at the doors,

but still, foes crushed his chronicles, contracts,
letters, hymns, myths and poems, then set fire

to the rest . . . thus baking them
to last and last and last.

Visiting Tombs at Alcobaça Abbey

After he exhumed her, he required the court
to kneel, kiss her decomposed hand,

then tore out her assassins' hearts.
He crowned her, declared her true queen

and designed two royal tombs.
Face-to-face they lie, Pedro and Inez,

effigies of fidelity-in-waiting positioned
"to the end of the world . . ." to rise

and, before the final judgment,
to greet one another first across the transept.

On his tomb, the king's incised narrative
of their love, royal lions recumbent beneath.

On hers, beauty, a rosary resting in long fingers,
Christ's life and the Judgment, her killers,

gargoyled, bent under marble weight,
and six trim angels attending her, two already lifting

her head, like his, expectant from its pillow.
Crossing the private space between their beds

stirs some unease, an urge to hurry,
and yet to bow, as before an altar.

At Ilium

Delivered to the ramparts
by a Turkish van,
I settle on a rubbly outlook
to populate the ruins –
Helen pacing the perimeter,
Trojan elders captured
by the sweep of her robes,
even as she sparks their final war.

In nearby fields, I place
Agamemnon's camp,
Achilles' sulky tent, and follow
ten bell-bottomed sailors
chasing one another
through dry grass, tooting tinny horns.

From the bastion where Astyanax
might have cried to his dying father,
I hear hootings, seamen happy
with escape from the sea, happy

with the dark-eyed girl who steps aside
on the narrow wall as they brush past,
who smiles as they shout to her
over ruins laid out flat at their feet.

Trojan Walls

daily compass Helen to the limits, where she circles
with no thought of escape to her husband,

dreading what he and his grievance have contrived,
and from where she watches elders watching her always,

they grateful to the seabreeze that undulates her robes,
and claiming to understand Paris's fatal urge to keep her.

She knows they see only Aphrodite's prize –
beauty's payoff gifted by beauty herself – but fail to see

Helen, who has no say in this – loveliness, marriage,
capture, bloody reclamation.

Not one of them knows if she would choose plainness,
her walks unnoticed, a fate her own,

nor does anyone know this cannot be, not with love's
goddess bound to a promise, Hera enraged yet again,

and Athena armed to destroy all things Trojan,
thus prompting her to watch, to spy ships approaching,

to spot Menelaus shading his eyes, seeking her
on the ramparts where she remains just now the Trojans'

to behold, Paris's in fact, certain to die
with the high towers' fall, so she paces the perimeter

of a doomed city, awaits return to her starting point –
where her captivating beauty will once more be enthroned,

her route again around
Spartan walls.

Burning Ghat, Burning Elephant

Among red jasmine petals,
Benares' Ganesha rests, draped
with leis of yellow marigold.

Elephant-headed with wisdom, big-eared
for the prayers, he is Lord of Beginnings,
here where the dying long for their last breath.

On biers of sandalwood, sparked by grasses,
the fortunate are set alight on Mother Ganges'
steps, and over hours, brains burst, and
charred fingers reach to heaven.

Prodded by Untouchables ungentle with poles,
they dissolve to smoldering ash and bone.

Flames reflect across the statue's big belly,
his four stone hands grayer in smoke,
the flowers, wrinkles in his trunk faded
into fine dust – a second incineration,
signing that all have done well.

Saint Nil's Crutches

No night, no day, no dusk, no dawn –
the only way was full-time prayer.

A demon clawing hellbound
was better than briefest sleeping, slothful.

He withdrew to mystic privacy,
leaned at a wall, propped on crutches

to catch him if he slipped senseless,
chanting the Jesus prayer.

His wooden statue captures the moment
of greatest resistance, spirit aloft,

body sinking to gravity –
beard flat on his breast resting,

brows like awnings, eyes closing down,
lidded, as during a litany,

hood, cape draping, fingers
over his knees, beads cascading

from beneath his hand. Crutches, alert,
lift his crumpling shoulders,

but sleeping's fare well threatens
all efforts against the fall.

To Carry on with the Dying

Vesuvio traced roads deep-rutted
by wagon wheels, crashed
lavish feasts in tendrilled gardens.
Ash tipped urns, mouths agape
for fresh red wine, surged into stables,
the forum, the palaestra, dried
the fountain where children shouted,
gossip whispered.

It claimed the *salve lucrum* mosaic,
hailing money, trespassed
the poet's snarling
cave canem warning,
twisted a chained dog
under tons of blackness.
Lives sprawled in their running
rested in place
for near seventeen centuries.

. . . until excavators, with care,
unearthed Apollo's sundial,
joyfully freed its shadow
to count down days again . . .

Now rain dissolves walls
portraying frescoed feasts,
unpaints, peels the pigment.

Pigeons roost and coo,
call the heights their own.

Sun bleaches color,
roots pry up roof-tiles
placed to protect each house,
finger down
into private chambers.
Lintels crumble.

Craving a memory,
tourists chip souvenirs.
Feral dogs hunt, howl,
prowl these rutted roads.

Five Kuznechny Lane

Wait, Fyodor. Don't hurry to hook
your black umbrella over your forearm
to don your shiny top hat
(now safely under glass)
for an escape alone down the Prospekt.

Take us, we ten a.m. tourists,
from this entry hall and
through your last apartment
where you wrote old Karamazov
into life, murdered him,
where you died of emphysema.

Pause at your desk (all potential now)—
the candles, unlit, the pen in its holder,
and let us learn how you could reach
so far from here.

Pass quickly the nursery
with its little girl's doll
and its sleek rocking horse,
maybe all too like your dead Alyosha's.

Here! Your samovar, for your perfect tea,
your favorite silver spoon.
No remarks on the cigarettes,

the prescription for your fading lungs,
the left-over medicine,
the clock frozen at 8:36.

You know, they've hung a life-sized copy
of Holbein's dead Christ, face contorted,
body pierced, mouth gaping,
long fingers darkening to decay, "a body,"
you wrote, "fully and entirely subject
to the laws of nature."

Come, Fyodor, why did you
climb a chair in Basel
to view more closely this agony—
your favorite painting,
but one that so disturbed you
your wife feared another seizure.

What was the appeal,
this cavernous Savior without breath?
So unlike your robust Sistine Madonna,
your glowing silver icon of the virgin,
the chalky peace of your own death mask.

Whirling with the Dervishes

Around the axis of their own
spines, they step into the whirl,
into the concentric ring of the wider

universal sphere, their white skirts
opening up, as arms crossed, turning,
turning, then with gentle centrifugality,

lift, one arm receiving celestial love,
the other reaching down and out to earth,
while reeds, strings, kettledrums join

the persistent lovesong of Rumi's
"Dance with me to heaven's tune,"
we sitting silent, following the turns,

the turns, the soft steps, the merging
of any one of them, then my choice
of one, counting the turns, one, two . . .

five hundred . . . turns . . . and like
the sleepy child I was, crossing
the country, counting, counting

the highway dash-lines, summers
with my parents, until the certain
turn at the Pacific, spinning on this

planet, loving them where I was,
where they were taking me, returning
me . . . have taken me.

Notes

Annie Oakley: Peerless Lady Wing-Shot: Annie Oakley (1860-1926) was in Buffalo Bill's Wild West Show for 17 years. She was the subject of the 1926 musical, "Annie Get Your Gun."

Red Cat, Clyde: In 2009, a cat named Clyde was returned from Cloncurry in the Australian Outback to his owner on the island of Tasmania. He had been missing three years and had traveled over two thousand miles.

Cleopatra's Conquest: In his *Natural History,* Pliny the Elder (23-79) tells of Cleopatra's bragging to Mark Antony that she could serve the most lavish meal ever, one worth the value of fifteen countries.

Jenny and Charles: Charles Darwin (1809-1882) visited Jenny, an orangutan, at the London Zoo in 1838.

Collectors: Horace Walpole (1717-1797) is best known for his gothic novel, *The Castle of Otranto.* His estate outside London housed his extensive collection of antiquities and artworks. Joseph Cornell (1903-1972), an American artist, created "assemblages," small glass-fronted boxes designed with objects discarded by others.

Annie Taylor Takes the Falls: Annie Taylor (1838-1921) was the first to go over Niagara Falls in a barrel, October 24, 1901.

Friday Night for Sale: Perry Como (1912-2001), a popular singer, had his own television show from 1956-1963. A Flexible Flyer was a wooden sled. In 1915, approximately 2,000 were purchased each day.

Methuselah: Methuselah, said to be 969 years old, is the oldest person named in the Hebrew Bible. Bristlecone pines have thrived in this California forest for 11,000 years.

Coins of the Realm: In the Medieval play, *Everyman*, the main character, Everyman, has simply accumulated wealth, never shared it, and so the character Goods refuses to accompany him to the afterlife. Sam Spade was writer Dashiell Hammett's hard-boiled detective.

Staffordshire Burial: In September 2009, an explorer with a metal detector discovered an Anglo-Saxon treasure buried in a Staffordshire field. At least fifteen hundred objects were excavated. Wealtheow is the wife of Hrothgar in *Beowulf.* The *comitatus* is the alliance of Anglo-Saxon warriors–lords and thanes. The *geldwine* is the "goldfriend," the lord who rewards bravery, seals alliances with lavish gifts. The *scop* is the bard, responsible for telling the tales, preserving the history.

En Paz Descanse: Robert Graves (1895-1985) was a prolific English writer, accomplished in many genres. EPD, often on Spanish gravestones, means "Rest in Peace."

The Library of Assurbanipal: Assurbanipal (668-627 BCE) was an Assyrian king who established a library at Nineveh. More than 20,000 tablets have survived.

Visiting the Tombs at Alcobaça Abbey: A fourteenth century love story between King Pedro I and Inez de Castro, set in Portugal.

Burning Ghat, Burning Elephant: In the Hindu pantheon, Ganesha is Lord of Beginnings.

Saint Nil's Crutches: Saint Nil Sorsky (1433-1508) was a Russian ascetic monk.

Whirling with the Dervishes: Rumi (1207-1273) founded the Mevlevi Sufi Brotherhood which performs their whirling dance as a route to spiritual ecstasy.

About the Author

Ann Taylor is a Professor of English at Salem State University in Salem, Massachusetts where she teaches surveys of English literature, Arthurian literature, courses on the essay, and many writing courses, including non-fiction and poetry writing. In addition to her many poetry publications, he has written two books on college composition and a collection of personal essays, *Watching Birds: Reflections on the Wing* (Ragged Mountain/McGraw Hill).

Acknowledgments

I would like to thank my husband, Francis Blessington, and my children, Geoff and Julia, for their patience and encouragement, Salem State University for sabbatical support and for the Colrain Conference, my students (two in particular, Lisa Hood and Christine Monahan for helping to set me on this path), members of my various workshops in Cambridge and in Concord, Mass., Professor Guy Rotella of Northeastern University, and my poet-mentors, Nadia Herman Colburn, Tom Daley, and especially Joan Houlihan.

Thanks also are due to the editors of the following publications for publishing versions of the included poems:

Appalachia: "Methuselah," "Tracings," "Only Annual," "The Lagoon." *Arion:* "Hypotenuses." *Aurorean:* "The River Within." *Avocet:* "The Prince Frog," "Let There Be Moose," "Campsite at Masai Mara." *Blue Unicorn:* "Saint Nil's Crutches." *Classical and Modern Literature:* "At Ilium," "Trojan Walls." *The Copperfield Review:* "Staffordshire Burial," "The Library of Assurbanipal," "To Carry on with the Dying." *Dalhousie Review:* "En Paz Descanse." *Del Sol Review:* "Annie Oakley: Peerless Lady Wing-Shot," "Cleopatra's Conquest," "Whirling with the Dervishes." *Ellipsis:* "Still Life with Empty Bowl." *Free Focus:* "Annie Taylor Takes the Falls." *Mobius:* "Finding the Hidden Meaning." *Pegasus:* "Cloaks, Italia," "So much of my journeying." *Pine Island Journal of New England Poetry:* "Julia's Leonids." *Red Owl:* "Take the Hills." *River Poet's Journal:* "Je ne sais quois." *Snowy Egret:* "Jenny and Charles." *The Unrorean:* "War Footage." *Utah English Journal:* "Spectral."